T0150316

FOREST GREEN

A Walk Through the Adirondack Seasons

FOREST GREEN

A Walk Through the Adirondack Seasons

by Liana M. Mahoney

illustrated by Maggie Henry

North Country Books, Inc.
Utica, New York

ISBN-10 1-59531-047-9
ISBN-13 978-1-59531-047-7

Design by Zach Steffen & Rob Igoe, Jr.

Library of Congress Cataloging-in-Publication Data

Mahoney, Liana.
  Forest green : a walk through the Adirondack seasons / by Liana
Mahoney ; illustrated by Maggie Henry.
    pages cm
  Summary: Illustrations and rhyming text introduce the reader to New
York State's Adirondack Mountains in each season of the year.
  ISBN 978-1-59531-047-7 (alk. paper)
  [1. Stories in rhyme. 2. Seasons--Fiction. 3. Nature--Fiction. 4. Adirondack
Mountains (N.Y.)--Fiction.] I. Henry, Maggie, illustrator. II. Title.
  PZ8.3.M2755For 2014
  E]--dc23
                        2014019887

North Country Books, Inc.
220 Lafayette Street
Utica, New York 13502
www.northcountrybooks.com

To Kerrigan, Liam, and McKenna, my favorite forest critters —L.M.

To Mom and Dad, thank you for all your love and support. —M.H.

You may have seen
The forest **green**
That paints the woodland's summer...

In needles of pine trees,
And hemlock, and fir;

Soft carpets of mosses,
And thick juniper.

In jack-in-the-pulpits,
And luna moths' wings,

The hum of cicadas;
Songs katydids sing...

In fall, instead,
The forest red
Paints the woodland's autumn...

On woodpeckers' faces,
And shiny chokecherries;

In foxes' thick fur;
In wintergreen berries.

In mushrooms and toadstools,
From decay, growing tall;

In maple leaves, scarlet,
Ablaze as they fall...

A wondrous sight,
    The forest white
Paints the woodland's winter...

With blanketed branches,
That droop heavy with snow;

And three-petaled trilliums
Lying dormant below.

In the stripes of the chipmunks
Asleep in their nests;

In the tail of the deer,
And the chickadee's breast...

With life anew,

The forest **blue**

Paints the woodland's spring...

In violets smiling
From patchwork bouquets;

And the sky framed by treetops

On clear, warming days.

In the eggshells of fledglings
That hatch, bald and lean,

In the robins' nests built
In the pines, forest green...